THE BIG ENCYCLOPEDIA OF DEFUNCT ANIMALS

VOLUME III

STANTON F. FINK

Acknowledgments

and Dedication

To my father, in whose books I discovered my first monsters.

To Will Caligan, whose help and encouragement is one of the primary reasons for this coloring book's existence.

To Mariano Silvera, who should have had his own artbooks

To Doctor David Morafka, who helped teach me to be more picky with my information.

To my friends, who helped push me to make this.

Table of Contents

Acknowledgments — page 2

Introduction — page 5

Glossary — page 6

Precambrian: *Eoandromeda octobrachiata* — page 8

Cambrian: *Capinatator praetermissus* — page 10

Ordovician: *Aristocystites bohemicus* — page 12

Silurian: *Ainiktozoon loganense* — page 14

Devonian: *Neoprobolium nasutus* — page 16

Carboniferous: *Barameda decepiens* — page 18

Permian: *Estemmenosuchus mirabilis* — page 20

Triassic: *Austrolimulus fletcheri* — page 22

Jurassic: *Uarbryichthys latus* — page 24

Cretaceous: *Koreaceratops hwaseongensis* — page 26

Paleocene: *Pucadelphys andinus* — page 28

Eocene: *Arfia shoshoniensis* — page 30

Oligocene: *Necronectes vidalianus* — page 32

Miocene: *'Samotherium' sinense* — page 34

Pliocene: *Persististrombus coronatus* — page 36

Pleistocene: *Elasmotherium sibiricum* — page 38

Holocene: *Chelychelynechen quassus* — page 40

Bibliography — page 42

About the Artist — page 45

Introduction

The purpose of this coloring book series is to provide information on various prehistoric animals both profoundly famous and incredibly obscure to artists of all ages. Of course, there is a lot of material to work with, as animals have been a major component of Earth's ecosystems for at least 670 million years.

For the sake of space and workability, each volume will contain 17 entries: ideally, one species for each geological time period, if possible. If you, or your inner and or outer child do not see your favorite prehistoric animal here, it may be eventually featured in another volume. Or, contact me at apokryltaros@gmail.com to have it put into a later volume.

Glossary

- **Aquatic**- Living in water.
- **Arthropod**- Any member of the animal phylum Arthropoda, including trilobites, arachnids, crustaceans, insects, myriapods and their relatives. All arthropods have armor-like, jointed exoskeletons made of chitin-derived plates, sometimes reinforced with calcium carbonate, and jointed limbs.
- **Breccia**- A form of sedimentary rock formed from a bunch of broken or uneroded rocks, or shells, or bones that have been cemented together.
- **Cambrian**- A period of time in the Paleozoic Era from 541 to 485 million years ago.
- **Carboniferous**- A period of time in the Paleozoic Era from 359 to 300 million years ago.
- **Cenozoic**- An era of time in the Phanerozoic Eon from 65 million years ago until now.
- **Chordate**- Any member of the animal phylum Chordata, including sea squirts, lancet fish, and vertebrates (such as lampreys, sharks, tuna, frogs, lizards, chickens, and people). All chordates have, at least at some point in their life cycle, a notochord, a long, flexible rod, usually made of cartilage, or, in the case of most vertebrates, cartilage and bone, running down the back from head to tail, directly beneath the neural tube.
- **Cnidarian**- Any member of the animal phylum Cnidaria, such as jellyfish, box jellies, Portuguese Man'o'war, sea anemones, coral and the parasitic myxozoans. Cnidarians are usually radially symmetrical, and have unique, venom-injecting stinging cells called "cnidocytes."
- **Cretaceous**- The last period of time in the Mesozoic Era, from 144 to 66 million years ago.
- **Devonian-** A period of time in the Paleozoic Era from 414 to 360 million years ago.
- **Ediacaran**- The last period of time in the Precambrian Eon from 635 to 542 million years ago.
- **Eocene**- A period of time in the Cenozoic Era from 55 to 33 million years ago.
- **Fauna**- In an ecological context, "fauna" refers to the animal components of an ecosystem.
- **Formation**- In a geological or paleontological context, a formation is a group of rock layers.
- **Gnathostome**- A gnathostome is any vertebrate chordate with a moveable jaw (or had an ancestor with one).
- **Holocene**- A period of time in the Cenozoic Era from 12,000 years ago until now.
- ***Incertae sedis***- A Latin phrase literally meaning "uncertain seat." *"Incertae sedis"* is a term in classification used to refer to a species or group whose relationships with related organisms are unclear or poorly defined.
- **Jurassic**- The second period of time in the Mesozoic Era, from 199 to 145 million years ago.

- **Mesozoic**- An era of time in the Phanerozoic Eon from 249 to 66 million years ago.
- **Miocene**- A period of time in the Cenozoic Era from 23 to 5 million years ago.
- **Mollusk**- Any member of the animal phylum Mollusca, including snails, clams, squid, octopuses, tusk shells and chitons. Most mollusks have a calcium carbonate shell, and a toothed, file-like tongue called a radula. All mollusks have a cape-like organ, the mantle, which usually secretes the shell, and houses breathing organs, and a nervous system.
- **Nekton**- Any aquatic animal that lives either entirely or almost entirely in the water column, and relies on its own swimming or propulsion abilities to keep and move itself in and around the water column. Anchovies, porpoises and ichthyosaurs are examples of nekton.
- **Neogene**- The second third of the Cenozoic Era, comprising of the Miocene and the Pliocene periods.
- **Oligocene**- A period of time in the Cenozoic Era from 33 to 23 million years ago.
- **Ordovician**- A period of time in the Paleozoic Era from 484 to 440 million years ago.
- **Paleocene**- A period of time in the Cenozoic Era from 65 to 55 million years ago.
- **Paleogene**- The first third of the Cenozoic Era, comprising of the Paleocene, Eocene, and Oligocene.
- **Paleozoic-** An era of time in the Phanerozoic Eon from 249 to 66 million years ago.
- **Permian**- The last period of time in the Paleozoic Era, the time of "The Great Dying," or most severe of all known extinction events, from 299 to 250 million years ago.
- **Pharynx**- A structure in the throat of many animals located directly behind the mouth or oral chamber. In vertebrates, it often houses breathing structures, like gills.
- **Plankton**- An organism that uses water currents and waterflow to as its primary means of transportation in the water column because it is either too small to move long distances by its own power, or lacks the ability to propel itself entirely. Sargassum seaweed and jellyfish are two varieties of plankton.
- **Pleistocene**- A period of time in the Cenozoic Era from 3 million years ago until 12 thousand years ago.
- **Pliocene**- A period of time in the Cenozoic Era from 5 to 3 million years ago.
- **Quaternary**- The last third of the Cenozoic Era, comprising of the Pleistocene and the Holocene periods.
- **Terrestrial**- Living on land.
- **Triassic**- The first period of time in the Mesozoic Era, from 249 to 200 million years ago.

Name *Eoandromeda octobrachiata*

Phylum

incertae sedis

Size

Diameter ranging from 1 to 4 centimeters

Time Period

Late Ediacaran of the Precambrian, 560 to 555 million years ago

Location

Denying Formation in the Yangtze Gorge, China, and Flinders Ranges, Australia.

Comments

Eoandromeda octobrachiata is a triangular, discoidal fossil with eight arm-like structures (hence the specific name) arranged in a spiral that reminded its describers of the Andromeda Galaxy (hence the generic name). It is thickest near the center, forming a gentle, mound-like peak so that the living creature would have looked something like a bun or a tam'o'shanter.

Exactly what *Eoandromeda* was, like the vast majority of Precambrian bugbears, is the subject of constant debate. Because the Denying Formation preserves several forms of algae and alga-like structures, it is suggested that *Eoandromeda* is an alga that grew with its eight stipes in a spiral. That *E. octobrachiata* is also preserved in the Ediacara Fauna of Australia, which does not appear to have any algae preserved, suggests it probably was an animal(-like organism). Some researchers have postulated it was a swimming organism related to comb jellies.

Name

Capinatator praetermissus

Phylum

Chaetognatha

Size

Body length up to 10 centimeters, grasping spines up to 1 centimeter in length.

Time Period

"Stage 3" of the Cambrian Period, 505 million years ago

Location

Walcott Quarry in Fossil Ridge, and other Burgess Shale localities, British Columbia.

Comments

Capinatator praetermissus is a very large chaetognath, or arrow worm from the Burgess Shale Lagerstatte, and is the second largest known chaetognath after the giant *Pseudosagitta gazellae*, a 12 centimeter monstrosity that eats krill.

C. praetermissus represents the stage in chaetognath evolution when chaetognaths were nektonic predators that swam near the seafloor, and before they became tiny, carnivorous zooplankton. It is thought to have lived near the seafloor as the majority of the 30+ fossil specimens are very well preserved, suggesting they were buried very quickly. The head of *Capinatator* is primarily a mouth flanked laterally by a set of 25 recurved, claw-like bristles (for a total of fifty). These claw-like bristles were used to seize prey and assist with shoving it through the mouth and into the gut.

Although *Capinatator* is the most primitive chaetognath known so far, it is not the earliest chaetognath. That title would go to the various Chengjiang Fauna chaetognaths, like *Eosagitta*. Paradoxically, the Chengjiang chaetognaths are small creatures more similar to modern chaetognaths.

| **Name** | *Aristocystites bohemicus* |

Phylum   Echinodermata

Class   Cystoidea

Order   Diplorita

Family   Aristocystitidae

Size   Theca/body about 1.5 to 2 centimeters wide at narrowest end, 3 to 5 centimeters wide at widest end, and 6 to 9 centimeters long.

Time Period   Late Caradocian Stage of the Late Ordovician

Location   Horné Zahorany, Bohemia, Czech Republic

Comments   *Aristocystites bohemicus* is a potato-shaped diploporite cystoid echinoderm from marine environments in what is now the Czech Republic during the Late Ordovician. Unlike many other diploporite cystoids, which tended to be shaped like a chicken drumstick, *Aristocystites* was shaped similar to a squat fingerling potato, covered in scale-like plates, and with a grate-like mouth on the wider end of the theca, or body. The mouth was laterally flanked on either end by a long, tentacle-like arm that probably housed tiny tube-feet that captured plankton and waterborne detritus. For over a century since its description by illustrious geologist Joachim Barrande in 1887, *Aristocystites* was thought to live on the seafloor with the narrower end of the theca stuck to or buried in the substrate. Recent findings now suggest that the living animal lay reclined on its side, like a miniature aristocrat's divan (or beanbag chair).

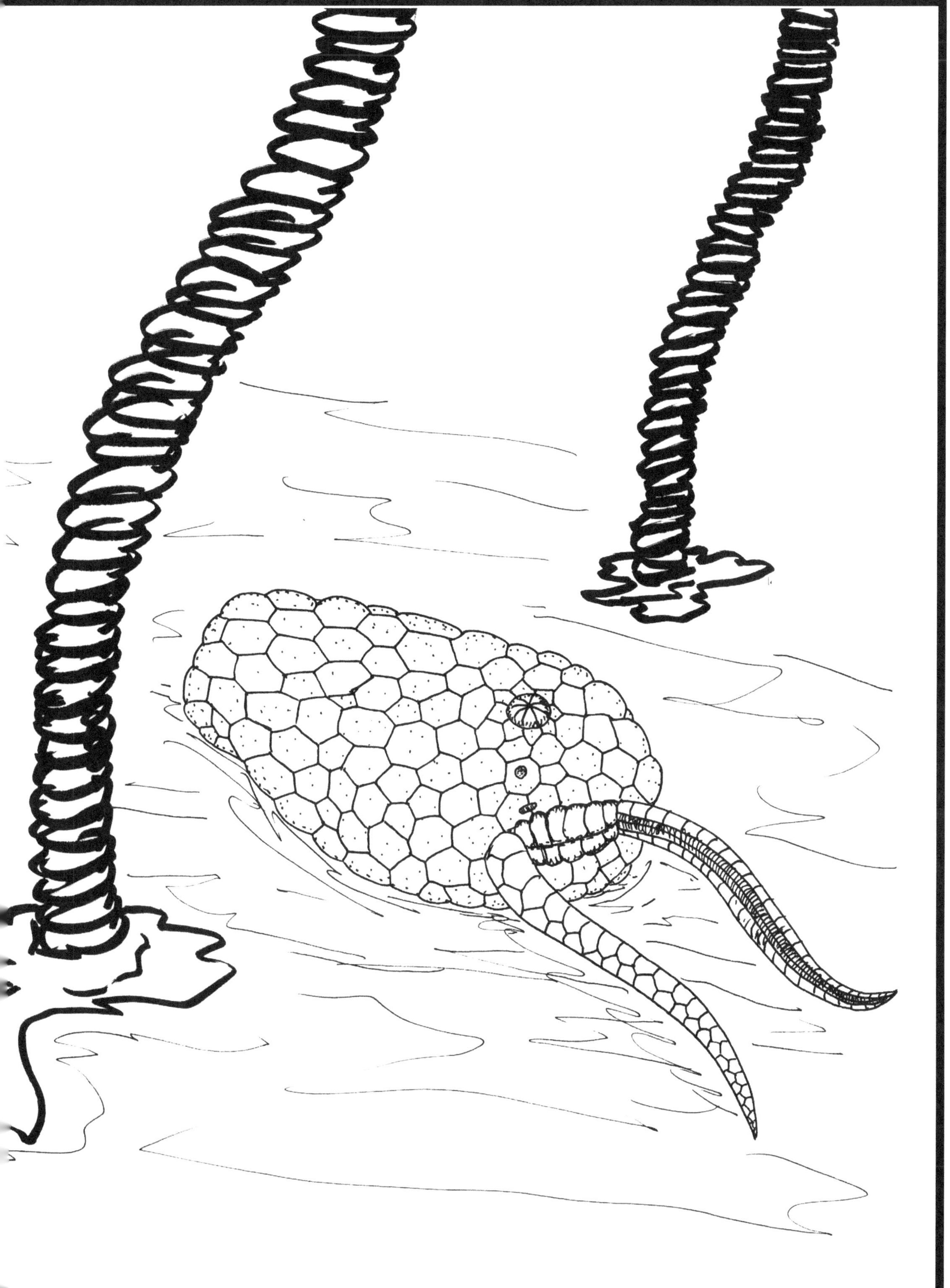

Name	*Ainiktozoon loganense*

Phylum   Arthropoda

Subphylum   ?Crustacea

Class   Thylacocephala

Order   Concavicarida

Size   From 2.5 to 24 centimeters from compound eye to the end of the tail

Time Period Llandovery Epoch of the Silurian, 444 to 428 million years ago

Location   *Jamoytius* Horizon of the Patrick Burn Formation, County of Lanarkshire, Scotland

Comments   When *Ainiktozoon loganense* was first described in 1937 (fifty years after the discovery of the first specimen in 1887), it was thought, with much reservations, thought to be some sort of bizarre chordate due to what were then assumed to be muscle striations in the tail. That it had what was apparently a compound eye made it wholly unlike any other chordate known. In 1997, a thorough reexamination proved that *Ainiktozoon* was a thylacocephalan arthropod, a member of an extinct group of arthropods tentatively identified as crustaceans (if only because thylacocephalans share more traits with crustaceans than they do with other arthropod groups). This identification was achieved when researchers realized it had many anatomical features in common with the Jurassic-aged *Dollocaris*, of France.

Ainiktozoon had a large, clog-shaped head-carapace, a prawn-like tail with little swimmerettes, and at least three pairs of raptorial limbs it used to seize prey it spotted with its large, vizor-like compound eye.

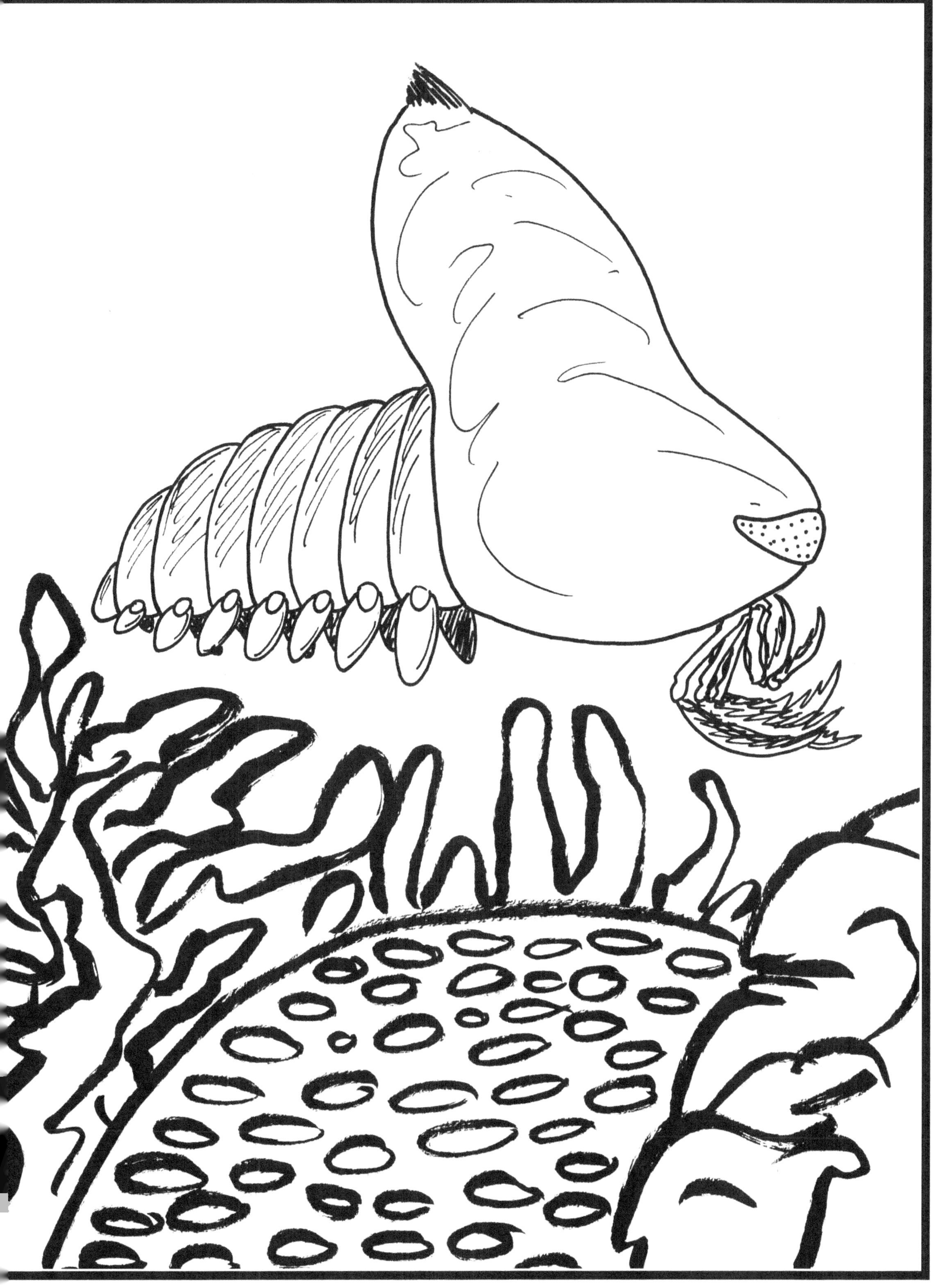

Name

Neoprobolium nasutus

Phylum	Arthropoda
Class	Trilobita
Order	Phacopida
Family	Dalmantidae
Size	Estimated length of the living adult animal probably up to 10 centimeters from glabellar "fork" to the tip of the pygidium spine.
Time Period	Lochkovian or "Helderbergian" epoch of the Early Devonian.
Location	New Scotland Limestone of Albany area, New York.
Comments	*Neoprobolium nasutus* is a large phacopid trilobite that lived in shallow sea reefs in what is now New York. It had a prominent "fork" that emanated from the anterior tip of its glabellum, and a long, needle-like spine emanating from the posterior end of its pygidium. The purpose of either are unknown. *N. nasutus* lived sympatrically with its relative, *N. tridens*: other species of *Neoprobolium* lived in similar Early Devonian reefs in what are now Oklahoma, France, and Siberia.

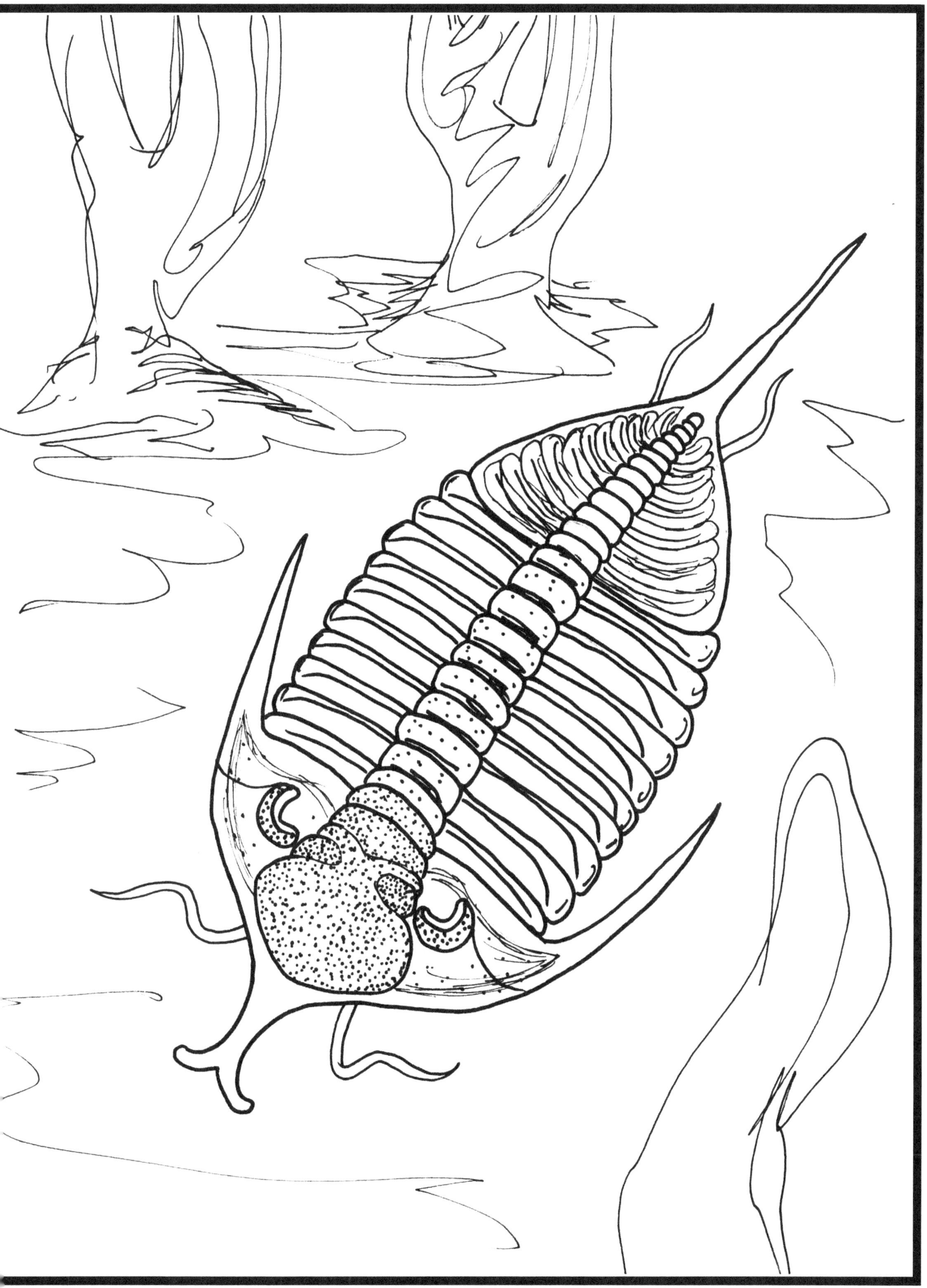

Name	*Barameda decepiens*

Phylum	Chordata
Class	Osteichthyes
Subclass	Sarcopterygii
Family	Rhizodontidae
Size	Adult length estimated to be up to 6.1 meters
Time Period	Tournasian Stage of the Early Carboniferous, 355 million years ago.
Location	The Mansfield Group, near the intersections of the Broken River and Ridge Creek, north of Mansfield, Victoria, Australia
Comments	*Barameda decepiens* is a very large to enormous rhizodontid lobe-finned fish from the early Carboniferous of Victoria, Australia. During the Late Devonian and Early Carboniferous, the region around what would become Mansfield, Victoria, was a swampy freshwater system filled with a diverse array of freshwater sharks, acanthodians, and lobe-finned fishes, including *Barameda*.

Barameda is regarded as closely related to, but more primitive than the later Carboniferous rhizodontid genera *Strepsodus* (in which *B. decepiens* was originally placed in), and *Rhizodus* (which grew even larger).

Barameda probably stalked or ambushed prey, grasping a victim with the long fangs in the forepart of its jaws, and thrashing about until the prey expired.

Name	*Estemmenosuchus mirabilis*
Phylum	Chordata
"Class"	Synapsida
Order	Therapsida
Suborder	Dinocephalia
Family	Estemmenosuchidae
Size	Skull up to 65 centimeters long, body estimated to be up to 300 centimeters long.
Time Period	Wordian Stage of the Middle Permian, about 267 million years ago
Location	Ezhovo Place near Perm, in the Ural Mountains of Russia.
Comments	*Estemmenosuchus mirabilis* is a large dinocephalian therapsid that lived in a floodplain in what would eventually become part of the Ural Mountains near Perm, Russia. *E. mirabilis'* frondose horns were derived from its frontal bones, and are thought to helped distinguish members of its own species from members of the related species, *E. uralensis*, which had horns that ended in knobs.

Although *E. mirabilis* had six pairs of sharp, pointed incisors, it is believed to be an herbivore. This is because its ponderously squat physique, coupled with its sprawling gait, makes the idea it could pursue prey an impossible fantasy. Instead, it probably tore out mouthfuls of vegetation to be swallowed.

Name	*Austrolimulus fletcheri*
Phylum	Arthropoda
Class	Merostomata
Order	Xiphosura
Family	Austrolimulidae
Size	Length from tip of caudal spine to anteriormost edge 14.6 centimeters; width from genal spine tip to genal spine tip 17.8 centimeters.
Time Period	Ladian Stage of the Middle Triassic, 238 to 240 million years ago.
Location	Beacon Hill shales, in the middle of the Middle Triassic-aged Hawkesbury Series in Brookvale, New South Wales.

Comments

Austrolimulus fletcheri is an extinct horseshoe crab from the Middle Triassic of New South Wales. It is best known for having long, sword-like genal spines that, coupled with the long caudal spine, gave the animal the resemblance of a clock pendulum or a miner's pickaxe.

In addition to its unusual appearance, arthropod specialists note that *Austrolimulus* represents a transitional form between horseshoe crabs of the family Belinuridae and Limulidae. In horseshoe crabs of the family Belinuridae, the segments of the opisthosoma (the hind-body that corresponds to the abdomen of arachnids, or the body and pygidium of trilobites) are distinct. In horseshoe crabs of the family Limulidae (including the still-living genera of *Limulus* and), the segments of the opisthosoma are fused together entirely into a single, mostly smooth unit. In *Austrolimulus* and its relatives, the segments of the opisthosoma are fused together, but still remain distinct.

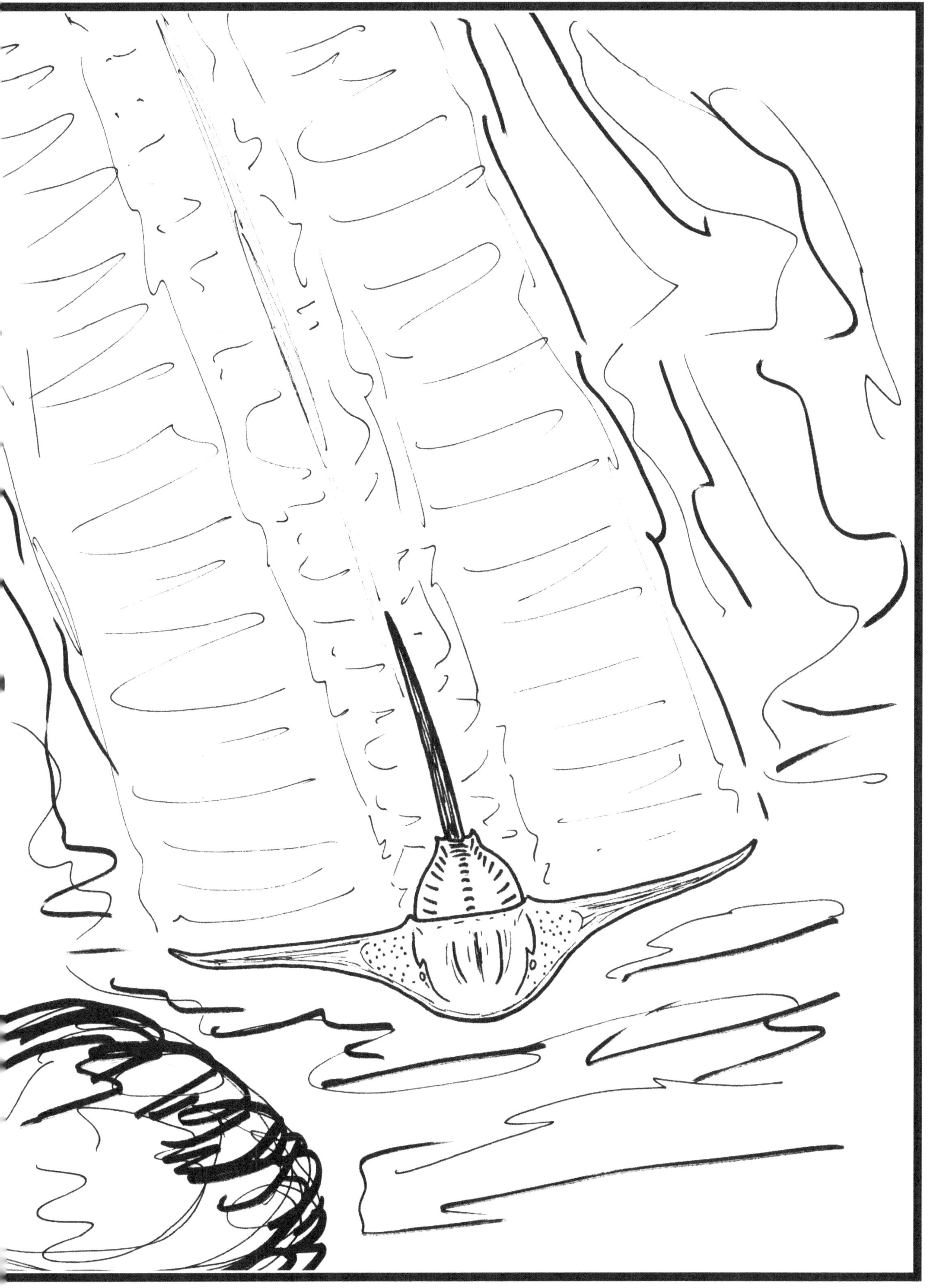

Name

Uarbryichthys latus

Phylum	Chordata
Class	Actinopterygii
Order	Macrosemiiformes
Family	Uarbryichthyidae
Size	Up to 26 centimeters
Time Period	Late Jurassic, about 175 million years ago.
Location	A lake in what is how the Talbragar Fishbeds in New South Wales, Australia

Comments

Uarbryichthys latus is a macrosemiiform fish from a lake or lake system in what is now the Talbragar Riverbed, New South Wales, Australia, when the entire continent was a region of Southeastern Gondwana. The lake had a diverse community of fish and plants, and was surrounded by an insect-filled forest. *U. latus* may have eaten insects blown into the lake, and smaller fishes.

U. latus was a superficially porgie-like fish that was originally described as a member of the extinct fish family Macrosemiidae on account of its similarity to some of that family's members. However, because *Uarbryichthys* does not have key features diagnostic of Macrosemiidae, it was then placed in its own family, Uarbryichthyidae. *U. latus*' living relatives include sturgeons, and bichirs.

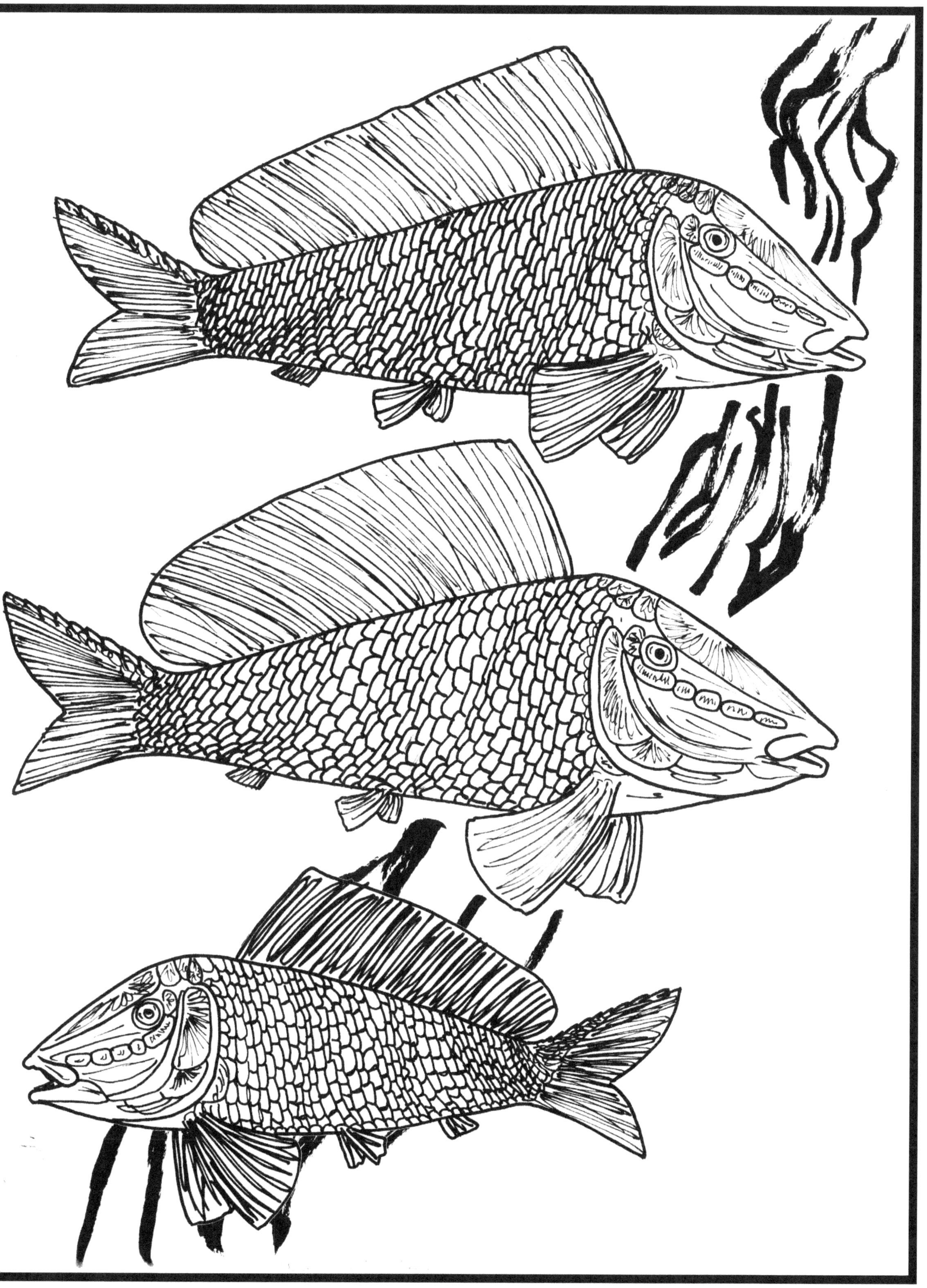

Name	*Koreaceratops hwaseongensis*

Phylum	Chordata
clade	Dinosauria
Order	Ornithischia
clade	Marginocephalia
Suborder	Ceratopsia
clade	Neoceratopsia
Size	Length of partial skeleton between 1.5 to 1.8 meters long, highest neural spine about 45 centimeters tall.
Time Period	Albian Epoch of the Early Cretaceous, about 103 million years ago
Location	Hwaseong City, South Korea
Comments	*Koreaceratops hwaseongensis* is a very small, basal neoceratopsian dinosaur from the Early Cretaceous of South Korea. The only known partial skeleton was found inside of a sandstone block incorporated into the Tando Dam near Hwaseong City.

The anatomy of the partial skeleton suggests *Koreaceratops* was closely related to both Leptoceratopsidae (i.e., *Asiaceratops, Leptoceratops,* and their relatives), and Coronosauria (i.e., *Graciliceratops, Protoceratops, Triceratops* and their relatives). The neural spines of the tail vertebrae are tall, giving the tail a paddle-like appearance. This, in turn, lead some researchers to hypothesize that *Koreaceratops* was adapted for swimming and or a semi-aquatic lifestyle.

Name	*Pucadelphys andinus*
Phylum	Chordata
Class	Mammalia
clade	Marsupialiformes
Family	Cretaoxyrhinidae
Size	Up to 30 centimeters with tail
Time Period	Tiupampan Stage of the Early Paleocene Period, 60 to 61.7 million years ago
Location	Santa Lucía Formation, Tiupampa, Bolivia

Comments

Pucadelphys andinus is a possum-like metatherian mammal from the Early Paleocene of Bolivia. *P. Andinus* was originally described as a marsupial in the possum family, Didelphidae. A 2016 study, however, places it as a non-marsupial closely related to the sparassodonts (i.e., *Borhyaena* and *Thylacosmilus*).

Several complete or nearly complete skeletons have been found in burrows. Researchers believe that the living animals dug out burrows along the banks of a river or an oxbow lake, and that, because each burrow was found occupied by two skeletons in "snuggling" positions, they lived as mated pairs. Because the burrows were filled up with sediment and debris, it is thought that these individuals of *P. andinus* were killed when a flashflood swept along the banks, filling their burrows up with mud.

Name   *Arfia shoshoniensis*

Phylum   Chordata

Class   Mammalia

Order   Creodonta

clade   Hyaenodonta

Family   Hyaenodontidae

Size   Probably similar in size to a Yorkshire terrier

Time Period   Wasatchian land stage of the Early Eocene, 55 to 50 million years ago

Location   Clarks Fork Basin, Wyoming

Comments   *Arfia shoshoniensis* is a species of small hyaenodontid creodont that lived in rainforests of what is now Wyoming. Several species of *Arfia*, all of which were small and dog-like, are found throughout North America and Eurasia from the Late Paleocene until the Early Eocene. Fossils from Late Paleocene and Early Eocene Mongolia suggest that the genus *Arfia* arose in Mongolia from Asian species of the hyaenodontid genus *Prototomus* during the Late Paleocene, and then emigrated from Mongolia into Europe, giving rise to at least two species there, and into North America, giving rise to seven species there (including *A. shoshoniensis*).

Fossils show that *A. shoshoniensis* lived together with the related hyaenodontid *Pyrocyon*. Stratigraphically, *A. shoshoniensis* would eventually be ecologically replaced by its immediate descendant, *A. opisthotoma*.

Name

Necronectes vidalianus

Phylum Arthropoda

Subphylum Crustacea

Class Malacostraca

Order Brachyura

Family Portunidae

Subfamily Necronectinae

Size Between one quarter of a kilogram to 1 kilogram in weight.

Time Period Middle Oligocene.

Location Near Biarritz, Bay of Biscay, France

Comments *Necronectes* is an extinct genus of portunid mud crab found in Oligocene-aged Atlantic/Tethys marine strata of the Iberian Peninsula, and Eocene to Miocene marine strata of the tropical New World. *Necronectes'* closest living relatives are the mud crabs of the genus *Scylla*, which are native to mangrove forests of the Indo-Pacific, and form fairly important aquaculture industries in Eastern Asia. Besides the fact that all species of *Necronectes* are all dead, species of *Necronectes* can be distinguished from species of *Scylla* (and from all other portunids) by how all species of *Necronectes* have eight pairs of spines along the lateral sides of their carapaces, with each species having their own unique arrangement of spines. *N. vidalianus'* spines, for instance, are more tightly packed than other *Necronectes* species.

Fossils of *N. vidalianus* are found in Middle Oligocene-aged marine limestones near Biarritz, a lovely villa in the Bay of Biscay, on the Atlantic coast of southern France. It probably lived either in mangrove mudflats similar to living *Scylla* mud crabs, or in shallow coastal waters very close to mangrove forests.

Name	*'Samotherium' sinense*

Phylum	Chordata
Class	Mammalia
Order	Artiodactyla
Family	Giraffidae
Subfamily	Samotheriinae
Size	Skull of the male up to 1 meter wide, from ossicone tip to ossicone tip.
Time Period	Late Miocene to Early Pliocene.
Location	Shanxi Province, China
Comments	*'Samotherium' sinsense* is a large giraffid artiodactyl mammal from the Late Miocene to Early Pliocene of Shanxi Province, China. In life, the animal would have looked like an enormous okapi with laterally pointing ossicones directly above the eyes. In the cow, the ossicones are short and stumpy. In the bull, the ossicones are long, slender, and horn-like.

'S.' sinense was originally placed in the genus *Samotherium* based on anatomical similarities with other species of *Samotherium*, especially with the species *S. neumayri* (now *Alcicephalus neumayri*). In a study sponsored by Donald Prothero, anatomical differences between *'S.' sinsense* and other species of *Samotherium* lead Prothero to suggest that *'S.' sinsense* be placed in its own genus. In a 2017 paper describing the newly discovered giraffid *Decennatherium rex* from Late Miocene Spain, this situation was confirmed in a tree that showed *'S.' sinsense* being the sister taxon of the subfamilies Samotheriinae and Sivatheriinae. Unfortunately, no giraffid researcher has yet to get around to officially remove *'S.' sinsense* from *Samotherium* and into its own genus.

Name

Persististrombus coronatus

Phylum	Mollusca
Class	Gastropoda
Superfamily	Stromboidea
Family	Strombidae
Size	Average adult shell lengths ranging between 8 to 12 centimeters long, exceptional individuals may be over 15 centimeters
Time Period	From the Tortonian stage until the Piacenzian stage, from the Late Miocene to Late Pliocene, 11.6 million to 2.58 million years ago.
Location	Altantic coast of Northwestern Africa, the Canary Islands, the Mediterranean Sea, Central Europe, the Balkan Peninsula.

Comments

Persististrombus coronatus is a long-lived species of large strombid conch snail that originated in the Atlantic of Western Africa during the late Miocene, and spread into (then) tropical Europe, becoming an important, if not dominant ecological component of Mediterranean shallow water environments until the cooling events at the end of the Pliocene drove *P. coronatus* into exinction by making the Mediterranean and the Atlantic African coast too cold.

The shell of *Persististrombus coronatus* is similar to that of the still-living Queen Conch, *Lobator gigas*, but smaller and having much larger, spike-like knobs around its spire. Aside from this, *P. coronatus* probably had a very similar lifestyle to *L. gigas*, crawling around sandy (underwater) meadows with a claw-like operculum, and feeding on algae in huge, herd-like groups. Whether or not *P. coronatus* housed a diverse mini-ecosystem of parasites and commensal symbiotes like the queen conch remains unknown. In many Pliocene marine strata of the Mediterranean, the shells are so numerous, they form breccias.

| **Name** | *Elasmotherium sibiricum* |

Phylum Chordata

Class Mammalia

Order Perissodactyla

Family Rhinocerotidae

Subfamily Elasmotheriinae

Size Skeletons suggest a height of over 2 meters at the shoulder, and a body length of 4 to 5 meters long. Weight estimated to be over 2,000 kilograms.

Time Period Middle to Late Pleistocene, from 700,000 to 29,000 or possibly 14,000 years ago.

Location Southwestern Russia, Western Siberia, Ukraine, and Moldova; possibly also Western Europe.

Comments If one ignores the rhinoceroses outside of Rhinocerotidae, then the second largest rhinoceros known is *Elasmotherium sibiricum*, from the Middle to Late Pleistocene. *E. sibiricum* easily dwarfed living rhinoceroses, and was surpassed in size only by its slightly larger immediate ancestor, *E. caucasicum*. The living *E. sibiricum* was a large, probably woolly-furred rhinoceros comparible in size to an elephant, and lived in the cold steppes of western Central Eurasia, and possibly France. An enormous dome on the skull was the base for a very large horn. The angle of the base of the skull demonstrates that the head could be held very close to the ground to enable grazing on grasses and other low-growing vegetation. The white rhinoceros, *Ceratotherium simum*, is the last living grazing rhinoceros; all other living rhinoceroses are browsers that feed on tree leaves and bushes.

Climatic changes near the end of the Pleistocene probably drove *E. sibiricum* into extinction.

Name

Chelychelynechen quassus

Phylum	Chordata
Class	Aves
Order	Anseriformes
Family	Anatidae
Size	Larger than a Canada goose.
Time Period	Early to Late Holocene, 12,000 to 1700 years ago
Location	Island of Kaui in the Hawaiian Archipelago

Comments

Chelychelynechen quassus, also known as the "Turtle-Jawed Moa-Nalo," "Kaui Moa-Nalo," and, in reference to its enormous size, the "Kaui Turtle-Jawed Goose," is the largest of the Moa-Nalo, (literally, "lost fowl"), a group of large, goose-like ducks that evolved from populations of the Pacific black duck, *Anas superciliosa*, that landed in the Hawaiian Archipelago soon after the islands arose in the Pacific Ocean at the start of the Holocene. The moa-nalo evolved their large sizes to browse on and more efficiently digest herbs and low-hanging vegetation, with different species having different-shaped beaks for specific niches. It is thought that many of the Hawaiian lobellias, *Cyanea sp.*, evolved large prickles to discourage moa-nalo from feeding on them. Moa-nalo probably competed with the indigenous geese, the Nēnē, *Branta sandvicensis*, the Nēnē-nui, *B. hylobadistes*, and the giant *B. rhuax*. Moa-nalo may have been preyed on by sea eagles, and, as ducklings, by harriers and owls.

C. quassus is known from bone fragments found in lava tubes in Kaui, hence the specific name *quassus* meaning "fragmented." These bone shards suggest an animal large as or larger than a large goose with a tall head, and a tall, serrated beak similar to that of a tortoise, hence the generic name translating as "turtle-lipped goose."

Here, a drake (standing) and a hen (seated) are compared with a mated pair of the insectivorous Kaui mole-duck, *Talpanas lippa.*

Bibliography

- Abdala, Fernando, Bruce S. Rubidge, and J. U. R. I. Van Den Heever. "The oldest therocephalians (Therapsida, Eutheriodontia) and the early diversification of Therapsida." *Palaeontology* 51.4 (2008): 1011-1024.
- Aguilera, Orangel A., and Alfredo A. Carlini, eds. *Urumaco and Venezuelan paleontology: The fossil record of the Northern Neotropics*. Indiana University Press, 2010.
- Ávila, Sérgio P., et al. "Persististrombus coronatus (Mollusca: Strombidae) in the lower Pliocene of Santa Maria Island (Azores, NE Atlantic): paleoecology, paleoclimatology and paleobiogeographic implications." *Palaeogeography, Palaeoclimatology, Palaeoecology* 441 (2016): 912-923.
- Briggs, Derek EG, and Jean-Bernard Caron. "A large Cambrian chaetognath with supernumerary grasping spines." *Current Biology* 27.16 (2017): 2536-2543.
- de Muizon, Christian. "A new carnivorous marsupial from the Palaeocene of Bolivia and the problem of marsupial monophyly." *Nature* 370.6486 (1994): 208.
- Fedonkin, Mikhail A., et al. *The rise of animals: evolution and diversification of the kingdom Animalia*. JHU Press, 2007.
- Feng, Tang, et al. "Octoradiate spiral organisms in the Ediacaran of South China." *Acta Geologica Sinica-English Edition* 82.1 (2008): 27-34.
- Feng, Tang, et al. "Eoandromeda and the origin of C tenophora." *Evolution & development* 13.5 (2011): 408-414.
- Frickhinger, Karl Albert. *Fossil atlas, fishes*. Mergus, 1995.
- Garvey, Jillian M., Zerina Johanson, and Anne Warren. "Redescription of the pectoral fin and vertebral column of the rhizodontid fish Barameda decipiens from the Lower Carboniferous of Australia." *Journal of Vertebrate Paleontology* 25.1 (2005): 8-18.
- Gingerich, Philip D. "Systematics and evolution of early Eocene Hyaenodontidae (Mammalia, Creodonta) in the Clarks Fork Basin, Wyoming." (1989).
- Givnish, T. J., et al. "Thorn-like prickles and heterophylly in Cyanea: adaptations to extinct avian browsers on Hawaii?." *Proceedings of the National Academy of Sciences* 91.7 (1994): 2810-2814.
- Goin, Francisco J., et al. "Phylogeny and Diversity of South American Metatherians." *A Brief History of South American Metatherians*. Springer, Dordrecht, 2016. 155-183.
- Harrington, H. J. "General description of Trilobita." *Treatise on invertebrate paleontology, Part O, Arthropoda* 1 (1959): 38-117.
- Harzhauser, Mathias, and Gijs C. Kronenberg. "The Neogene strombid gastropod persististrombus in the Paratethys Sea." *Acta Palaeontologica Polonica* 58.4 (2013): 785-802.
- Ivakhnenko, M.F. (2000). "*Estemmenosuchus* and primitive theriodonts from the Late Permian". *Paleontological Journal*. **34** (2): 184–192.
- Kosintsev, P. A. "Elasmotherium sibiricum Fisher (1808). New data on the Period of

existence and geographic range." *The Quaternary of the Urals: Global Trends and Pan-European Quaternary Records, UrFU, Ekaterinburg* (2014): 67-68.

- Kohn, Alan J. "Treatise on Invertebrate Paleontology, Part I, Mollusca 1." (1962): 68A-70A.
- Lee, Yuong-Nam; Ryan, Michael J.; Kobayashi, Yoshitsugu (2011). "The first ceratopsian dinosaur from South Korea". *Naturwissenschaften.* **98** (1): 39–49.
- Long, John A. "A new rhizodontiform fish from the Early Carboniferous of Victoria, Australia, with remarks on the phylogenetic position of the group." *Journal of Vertebrate Paleontology* 9.1 (1989): 1-17.
- MOORE, R, (Ed.), Treatise on Invertebrate Paleontology, Part R (Arthropoda 4, Vol. 1)
- Olson, Storrs L., and Helen F. James. "Descriptions of thirty-two new species of birds from the Hawaiian Islands: Part I. Non-Passeriformes." *Ornithological Monographs* 45 (1991): 1-88.
- Parsley, Ronald L. "Aristocystites, a recumbent diploporid (Echinodermata) from the Middle and Late Ordovician of Bohemia, ČSSR." *Journal of Paleontology* 64.2 (1990): 278-293.
- Prothero, Donald R., and Scott E. Foss, eds. *The evolution of artiodactyls*. JHU Press, 2007.
- Riek, E. F. "A NEW XIPHOSURAN FROM THE TRIASSIC SEDIMENTS AT BROOKVALE, NEW SOUTH WALES." Records of the Australian Museum 23 (1955): 281-282
- Ríos, María, Israel M. Sánchez, and Jorge Morales. "A new giraffid (Mammalia, Ruminantia, Pecora) from the late Miocene of Spain, and the evolution of the sivathere-samothere lineage." *PloS one* 12.11 (2017): e0185378.
- Ritchie, Alexander. "Ainiktozoon loganense Scourfield, a protochordate? from the Silurian of Scotland." *Alcheringa* 9.2 (1985): 117-142.
- Scourfield, D. J. "An anomalous fossil organism, possibly a new type of chordate, from the upper silurian of lesmahagow, lanarkshire—Ainiktozoon loganense, gen. et sp. nov." *Proc. R. Soc. Lond. B* 121.825 (1937): 533-547.
- Schvyreva, A. K. "On the importance of the representatives of the genus Elasmotherium (Rhinocerotidae, Mammalia) in the biochronology of the Pleistocene of Eastern Europe." *Quaternary International* 379 (2015): 128-134.
- Taviani, M. A. R. C. O. "Unpersisting Persististrombus: a Mediterranean story." *Vieraea* 42.9 (2014): e18.
- Turner, Alan. *National Geographic Prehistoric Mammals*. National Geographic, 2004.
- Van Der Brugghen, Wim, Frederick R. Schram, and David M. Martill. "The fossil Ainiktozoon is an arthropod." *Nature* 385.6617 (1997): 589-590.
- Walther, Michael, and J. P. Hume. "Extinct birds of Hawaii." *Honolulu, HI: Mutual Publishing* (2016).
- Wilson, Gregory P., et al. "A large carnivorous mammal from the Late Cretaceous and the North American origin of marsupials." *Nature communications* 7 (2016): 13734.
- Whiteley, Thomas Edward, Gerald J. Kloc, and Carlton Elliot Brett. *Trilobites of New York: an illustrated guide*. Ithaca, NY: Cornell University Press, 2002.

About the Artist

Stanton F. Fink is a student of Biology and Chinese Medicine, and makes a hobby of drawing monsters and researching flowers, arcane-looking creatures, prehistoric animals, fish, reptiles, birds and the occasional, really grotesque fungal fruiting body.

Stanton grew up and went to school in California and is currently living, drawing, and gardening in Oregon.

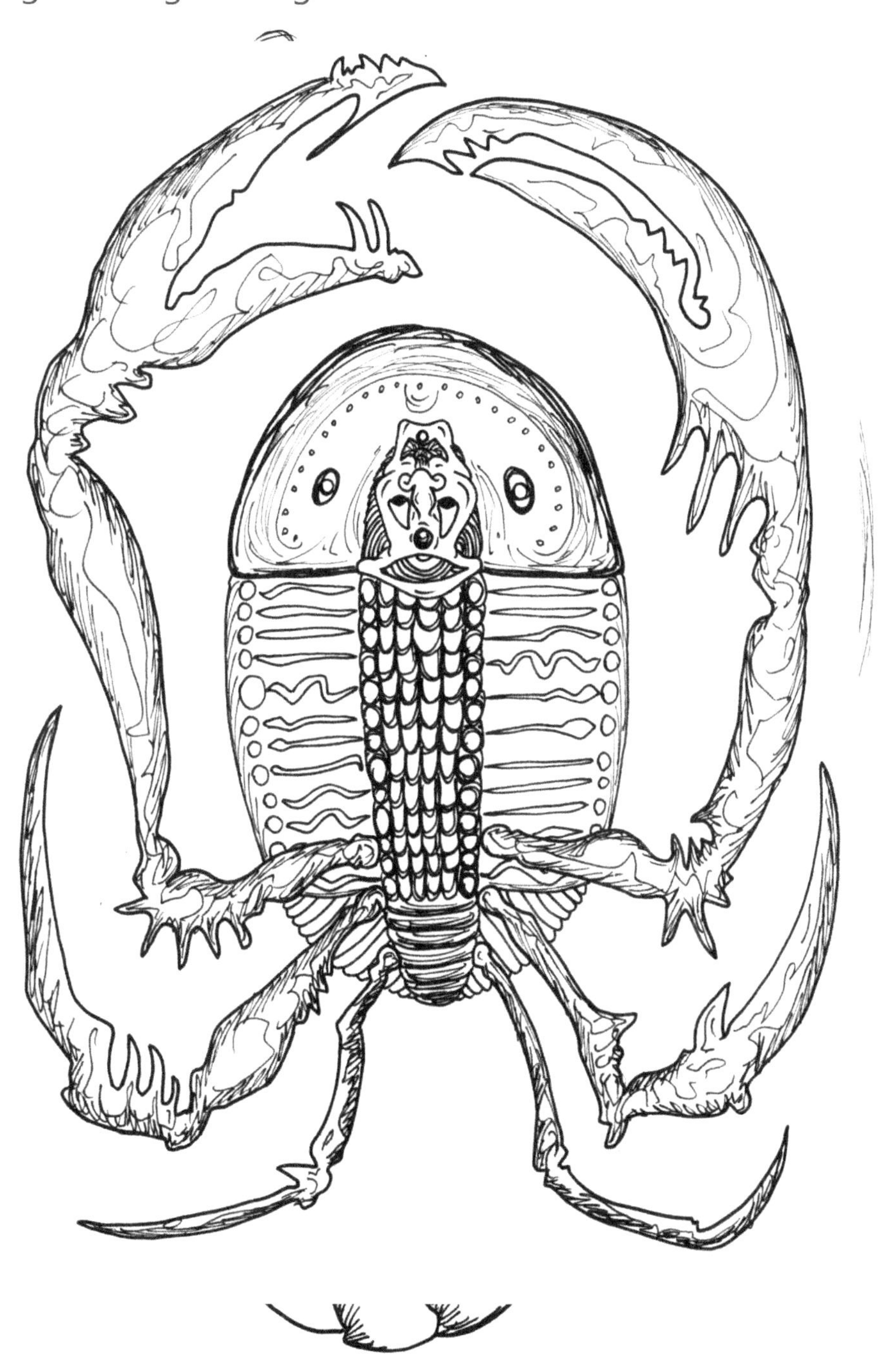